W9-ABU-109

J 595.799 WOO
Woodward, John,
Bee /

BEE

John Woodward

CHELSEA
CLUBHOUSE
An Imprint of Chelsea House Publishers

Bee

Chelsea Clubhouse
An imprint of Chelsea House
132 West 31st Street
New York, NY 10001

Library of Congress Cataloging-in-Publication Data
Woodward, John, 1954-
  Bee / John Woodward.
    p. cm. -- (Garden minibeasts up close)
  Includes bibliographical references and index.
  ISBN 978-1-60413-901-3
  1. Bees--Juvenile literature. I. Title. II. Series: Woodward, John, 1954- Garden minibeasts up close.
  QL565.2.W66 2010
  595.79'9--dc22

                    2010004407

Produced for Chelsea House by Discovery Books
Managing Editor: Laura Durman
Project Editor: Clare Collinson
Designer: Blink Media
Illustrator: Stuart Lafford

Photo acknowledgments: FLPA: pp 15 (Michael Durham/Minden Pictures), 16 (Mark Moffett/Minden Pictures), 20 (Heidi & Hans-Juergen Koch/Minden Pictures), 22 (Treat Davidson), 24 (Mark Moffett/Minden Pictures), 25 (Heidi & Hans-Juergen Koch/Minden Pictures); Getty Images: pp 8 (Steve Hopkin), 19 (Oxford Scientific); iStockphoto.com: pp 4 (Can Balcioglu), 5 (Alexey Kryuchkov), 9 (Peter Miller), 11 (Pauline S. Mills), 12 (Christopher Badzioch), 18 (stachu343), 21 (James Figlar), 26 (Eric Delmar); osf.co.uk: p 13 (Satoshi Kuribayashi/Nature Production); Shutterstock Images: title page (abxyz), pp 7 (André Gonçalves), 10 (Lepas), 14 (Bill Kennedy), 17 (Florin Tirlea), 23 (Veronika Trofer), 27 (Fred Leonero), 28 (Kirsanov), 29 top (PeJo), 29 bottom (barbaradudzinska).

Cover printed by Bang Printing, Brainerd, MN
Book printed and bound by Bang Printing, Brainerd, MN
Date printed April 2010
Printed in the United States of America

10 9 8 7 6 5 4 3 2 1

Contents

Finding bees

Sometimes you can hear a bee before you see it! Bees are flying insects that buzz from flower to flower, collecting **nectar** and **pollen**. They can be found wherever there are flowering plants.

The best time to look for bees is in the spring and summer, when there are lots of flowers.

Did You Know?

Bees appeared on Earth about 100 million years ago, during the age of dinosaurs. Before then there were no flowers, so there was no nectar for bees to collect.

Like other bees, bumblebees can often be seen gathering nectar and pollen from flowers.

There are more than 3,500 different kinds of bees in the United States. One of the best known is the honeybee. You may also have seen big, furry bumblebees in your backyard.

A bee's body

Would you know a bee if you saw one? Bees have furry bodies. Often, they have black and yellow or orange stripes. They have six legs, two pairs of wings, and a long tongue for sucking up nectar.

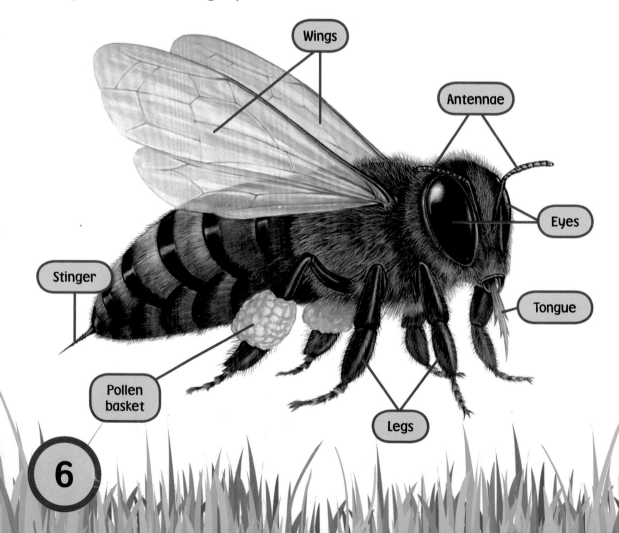

Wings

Antennae

Eyes

Tongue

Stinger

Pollen basket

Legs

6

A bee uses its antennae mainly to smell and taste. The antennae also help the bee feel its way around.

On its head, a bee has shiny black eyes and two **antennae**, or feelers. Some bees have special "pollen baskets" on their back legs. They use them for carrying pollen. Most bees have sharp **stingers**.

Did You Know?

Bees are closely related to wasps and look very much like them. But bees have more fur than wasps. Bees are also less likely to sting you!

Queens and colonies

Honeybees and bumblebees live in large groups called **colonies**. There are three different kinds of bee in the colony. Each type of bee has its own job to do.

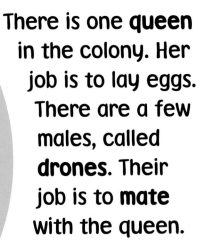

Queen bee

There is one **queen** in the colony. Her job is to lay eggs. There are a few males, called **drones**. Their job is to **mate** with the queen.

The queen is the largest bee in the colony. A queen honeybee may live for five years or more.

Most members of the colony are **worker bees**. Workers are females, but they cannot lay eggs.

Worker bees have lots of jobs to do. They build a nest for the colony, collect nectar and pollen, and make honey. Workers also take care of the young and feed the queen.

Worker bees are the smallest in the colony. They usually live for only a few weeks.

9

Nests and honeycomb

Wild honeybees often make their nests in hollow trees or logs. If you see a honeybee's nest, you should stay away. But if you could look inside, you would be amazed at its beautiful design.

Inside the nest, there are rows of six-sided **cells**, forming a **honeycomb**.

Honeycomb cells are made from wax produced by worker bees. The bees use the cells for storing honey and pollen and for raising young bees.

Bumblebees sometimes build their nests on the ground and cover the entrances with grass, mud, or leaves.

Bumblebee colonies often live underground in holes dug by other animals. Bumblebees also build their nests in walls and hollow trees, or in long grass on the ground.

Inside their nests, bumblebees make cup-shaped wax cells for storing eggs and a wax "honeypot" for storing honey.

Solitary bees

Not all bees live in colonies like honeybees and bumblebees. Most kinds of bees are **solitary**. There are no queens or workers, and each female builds her own small nest.

Some solitary bees dig holes in the ground. Others build their nests in cracks in walls or trees. They line their nests with mud or leaves.

Like many solitary bees, this digger bee has made its nest in a hole in the ground.

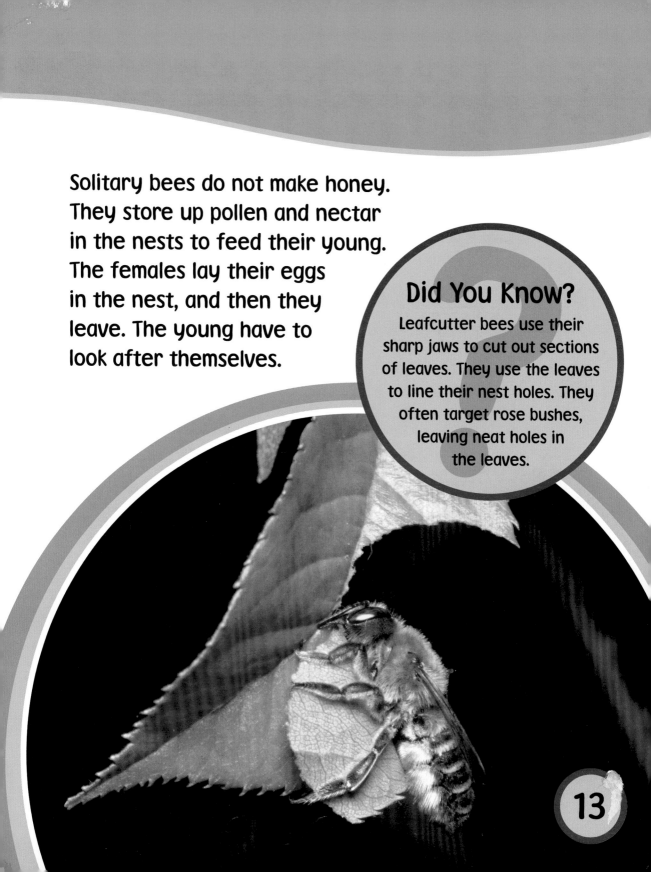

Solitary bees do not make honey. They store up pollen and nectar in the nests to feed their young. The females lay their eggs in the nest, and then they leave. The young have to look after themselves.

Did You Know?

Leafcutter bees use their sharp jaws to cut out sections of leaves. They use the leaves to line their nest holes. They often target rose bushes, leaving neat holes in the leaves.

Collecting food

Did You Know?

Bees sometimes fly up to 5 miles when they are gathering food. Their top speed is about 15-20 miles per hour!

Have you ever seen a busy bee flying from one flower to the next? The bee dips its long tongue into each bloom and sucks up the nectar.

The sugary nectar gives the bee **energy**. The bee also stores nectar in the special "honey stomach" in its body and takes it back to the nest.

A single bee may have to sip nectar from as many as 1,500 flowers to fill its honey stomach. After taking the nectar back to the nest, it will come out again for more.

Tongue

Pollen basket

When a bee has filled its pollen baskets, it takes the pollen back to the nest. The pollen is fed to the young bees in the colony.

When a bee visits a flower, grains of pollen stick to the hairs on its body. Honeybees and bumblebees pack the pollen into the pollen baskets on their back legs.

Did You Know?

Some bumblebees can carry up to half their own weight of pollen in their pollen baskets.

Making honey

You probably love the taste of honey, but have you ever wondered how it is made? Honeybees and bumblebees make honey from the nectar they collect from flowers.

Nectar is mostly a mixture of sugar and water. It begins to turn into honey when bees chew it.

A bee sucks nectar from another bee's honey stomach. The bee chews the nectar to help turn it into honey.

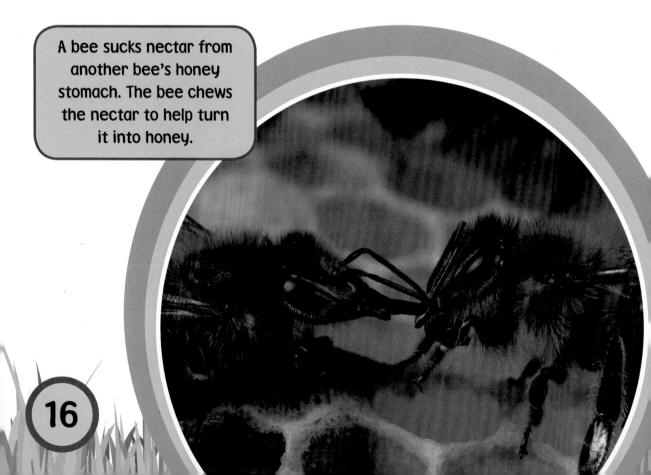

Wax seal

Honey

Honey provides food for young bees. It also feeds the colony through the winter when there is no food available from flowers.

When bees chew nectar, the mixture loses some of its water. It begins to thicken. The bees then put the mixture in the honeycomb cells. They fan their wings to help it dry out. As it dries, it becomes thick, gooey honey.

Did You Know?

A colony of honeybees must visit about 2 million flowers and fly about 55,000 miles to make just 1 pound of honey!

When the honey is ready and the cells are full, the bees seal them up with wax.

Eggs and young

Each year in spring, queen honeybees start to lay eggs. They place each egg in a honeycomb cell in the nest. After a few days, the eggs hatch into **larvae**.

Bee larvae do not look at all like adult bees. They are small and white, and they have no eyes, legs, or wings.

Larva

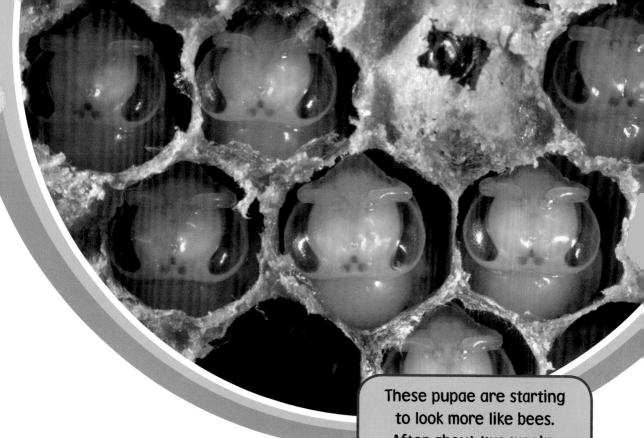

These pupae are starting to look more like bees. After about two weeks, they will change into adult bees and push their way out of the cells.

For the first few days, worker bees feed larvae on a special food called "royal jelly." Then the larvae are given pollen and honey.

The larvae grow quickly. After a few weeks, they turn into **pupae**. Then they change into adult bees.

Did You Know?

Royal jelly is a special food made by bees. It is given to the queen and to newly hatched larvae. If a larva is fed only on royal jelly, it will become a new queen.

19

Swarms

Honeybees survive the cold winter months by feeding on the honey they have stored in their nest. In spring, as new bees are born, the nest can become overcrowded.

When this happens the queen sometimes leaves the nest. She takes a big group of workers called a **swarm** with her.

A swarm of bees may look frightening, but swarming bees do not usually attack people unless they are threatened. If you see a swarm of bees, just walk away slowly.

After leaving the nest, the swarm settles somewhere for a few days. Then the bees move to a new nest site where they start another colony. The old nest is taken over by a new, young queen.

If you see a large group of honeybees clinging to a tree, don't panic. They are just moving house!

Stinging defense

Have you ever been stung by a bee? Bees often have sharp stingers in their tails, a bit like needles.

Only female bees have stingers. They use them to inject **venom** into an enemy, causing a sharp pain.

Beekeepers who keep bees in artificial beehives wear protective clothing to avoid being stung.

Bees that are collecting pollen and nectar rarely sting. Bees usually only sting to defend their nests or when they are frightened.

Did You Know?

A few people are **allergic** to bee stings. They become very ill if they are stung and need immediate treatment. Luckily, allergies to bee stings are rare.

Bee language

If you discover something good, how do you tell others about it? Honeybees do it by dancing! When a worker bee finds a good source of nectar, it returns to the nest. Then it performs a dance to show the other bees where the flowers are.

A group of bees have gathered around a dancing bee to find out where the nectar is.

Dancing bee

24

This bee is laying a scent trail to help other workers find the flowers it has discovered.

Bees also **communicate** with each other by producing powerful scents, or smells. The scents can carry different messages. One scent raises an alarm, attracting other workers to sting anything that attacks the nest.

Pollination

As a bee gathers nectar and pollen, it carries pollen from one flower to the next. The pollen **fertilizes** the flowers, which makes them produce seeds. This process is called **pollination**.

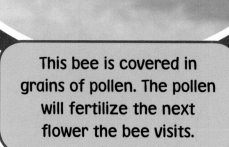

This bee is covered in grains of pollen. The pollen will fertilize the next flower the bee visits.

Pollination enables new plants to grow. Without it, there would be no new plants.

Bees are important because they pollinate farm crops and fruit trees. Other insects also pollinate crops, but bees do it best. This is because each bee visits hundreds of flowers every day.

Beekeepers often move their beehives from one farm to another so the bees can pollinate the farmers' plants.

Bees and people

Did you know that honeybees are the only insects that make food that people eat? People have been keeping bees for their honey for at least 3,000 years.

Bees in artificial beehives build their honeycombs in wooden frames. The beekeeper can lift each frame out and remove the honey.

Did You Know?

Honey stored in sealed jars can stay edible for hundreds of years! It doesn't rot like other foods—although really old honey may not have much flavor.

People have also used beeswax for thousands of years. Nowadays, it still has many uses. It is often used for making candles, as well as in ointments, skin creams, and furniture polish.

Beeswax candles have a nice smell and do not produce any smoke.

Glossary

allergic: Being very sensitive to and made ill by something that does not affect other people so badly.

antennae: The "feelers" on the head of an insect, which it uses to feel its way around and to pick up smells.

artificial beehive: A nest for honeybees made by humans.

barbed: Having a sharp spike, angled like a hook.

cell: In a bees' nest, a small container made of wax.

colony: A group of animals that live together.

communicate: To pass on information.

drone: A male bee, whose only job is to mate with a queen.

energy: The ability to do active things.

fertilize: In plants, to add the male cell to a female cell so that a seed develops.

honeycomb: Wax cells made by honeybees for storing honey, pollen, eggs, and larvae.

larva: The young life stage of an insect.

mate: When males and females come together to produce young.

nectar: The sugary liquid produced by flowers.

pollen: Tiny grains produced by flowers.

pollination: When pollen is carried from one flower to another. The pollen fertilizes the flower so it can develop seeds.

pupa: In bees, a young form of a bee, between larva and adult.

queen: In a colony of bees, a female that is able to produce eggs.

solitary: In bees, living alone in a small nest rather than in a large colony.

stinger: The part of a bee or other insect that holds its sting.

swarm: A large number of bees that leave their nest to find a new nest.

venom: A poison that is used by animals to kill their prey or defend their nest.

worker bee: A female bee that builds the nest, gathers food, and cares for the young bees. Worker bees cannot lay eggs.

Further resources

Books

Franks, Katie. *Bees Up Close.* New York: PowerKids Press, 2008.
An interesting look inside the bee's world.

Hartley, Karen, and Chris Macro. *Bee.* Chicago: Heinemann, 2006.
This book answers common questions about bees, such as "Why do bees buzz?"

Rotner, Shelley, and Anne Woodhull. *The Buzz on Bees: Why are they disappearing?* New York: Holiday House, 2010.
Bees are disappearing at an alarming rate. This book looks at possible explanations for bees' disappearance, what scientists are doing to address the problem, and also what young readers can do.

Slade, Susan. *Bees.* New York: Rosen Publishing, 2008.
An information-packed look at the bees that live in your backyard.

Thomson, Ruth. *A Bee's Life Cycle.* New York: PowerKids Press, 2010.
Find out about all of the stages in the life cycle of a bee.

Twist, Clint. *Honeybees.* New York: Gareth Stevens Publishing, 2006.
Explore the amazing world of the hardworking honeybee.

Web sites

Everything About: Bees, *http://www.everythingabout.net/articles/biology/animals/arthropods/insects/bees*
A useful Web site with information devoted to different types of bees, honey, and beekeeping.

Honey Bee Mystery, *http://kids.nationalgeographic.com/Stories/AnimalsNature/Honey-bee-mystery*
Find out why bees across the United States are flying away from their beehives and dying.

Pestworld for Kids, *http://www.pestworldforkids.org/bees.html*
Learn about different types of bees, what they eat, what they look like, and where you might find them.

Urban Bee Gardens, *http://nature.berkeley.edu/urbanbeegardens*
A useful page by the University of California about creating a bee-friendly habitat in your backyard.

Hey! A Bee Stung Me!, *http://kidshealth.org/kid/ill_injure/bugs/bee.html*
A Web page that explains what to do if you are stung by a bee, and how to reduce the risk of being stung.

Index